C#

FOR BEGINNERS

TABLE OF CONTENTS

INTRODUCTION

In today's world (IT) is all pervasive, everywhere, and in every facet of our day to day life. Prominently service sector involving railway, airlines, scientific and businesses establishments, banks, universities, schools, and most definitely in our homes. The phrase 'information technology' has many varying connotations in the same way as it has a wide spread presence.

From the most mundane of things which a common person does to the most complex wizardry which only a techno savvy geek comprehends. Information technology can be seen and experienced in processes improving services to citizens and consumers (online transactions, bookings, university admissions, professional consultations, telecommunications, consumer products etc), increasing the productivity and efficiency of governments (computerization of government records, departments, e-cops).

It also strengthens the legal and law enforcement systems (Judicial administration and Court Management) and in promoting the priority economic sectors (banking, agriculture, industry, marketing and the like), involving processes of manufacturing and production chain. Possibly the greatest impact Information technology has had is on blurring the time and geographical divide.

The penetration of the home computer or the personal computer phenomenon along with the Internet has increased the impact of information technology beyond our own imagination. Thus use of Internet has given the globe a shrinking effect. Every kind of information is only a few clicks away. In today's world of competition -"information" is the key word to success.

Availability of right information at the right time can make all the difference. Today relevant information outweighs the price of gold. The graphical user interface has simplified one of the most complex issues in the world. Indeed, the world is undergoing a second Industrial Revolution.

Information technology today touches every aspect of life, irrespective of location on the globe. Everyone's daily activities are affected in form, content and time by the computer. Businesses, Governments and individuals all receive the benefits of this Information Revolution. While providing tangible benefits in time and money, the computer has also had an impact on everyday life, as computerized routines replace mundane human tasks.

More and more of our businesses, industries, economies, hospitals and Governments are becoming dependent on computers. With the computer, the heretofore impossible has now become possible, The computer has allowed large volumes of data to be reduced to high-density, compact storage, nearly imperceptible to the human senses. It has allowed an exponential increase in speed, and even the most complex calculations can be completed in milliseconds. The miniaturization of processors has permitted worldwide connectivity and communication.

CHAPTER 1

INFORMATION TECHNOLOGY

Around one hundred and fifty years ago, businesses ran their day to day operations completely different from what businesses of the modern era do to run their day to day operations. People back then worked under candle light doing math calculations on paper, the old fashion way, before electricity came about in the early 20th century.

Now, most of the civilized world wouldn't know what to do with themselves without technology. Imagine not even having a calculator for math or the internet to do research. Yes, I know, it is hard to believe people were able to survive without these advanced tools that we take for granted each day.

The advances in communication combined with the evolution of the IT industry has made it possible for people to do business throughout the world in real time. Improvements in IT improve our lifestyles and business by allowing computers to reduce complications and enrich possibilities.

These days, the name "Information Technology" has managed to encompass many aspects of computer technologies invented in the past couple decades. These IT spectrums can be covered in many types of professional fields such as Management Information Systems, Computer Networking, and Software Design. Our ancestors couldn't even fathom what our society has accomplished.

In medicine, Information Technology also plays a substantial roll. Doctors take pictures with machines like a computerized axial tomography (CAT) or magnetic resonance imaging (MRI) and can print out three dimensional images of bones, muscles, and organs. These images can help map out patient's problems and help save lives. This day and age, it is difficult to find a field or industry that IT has not been greatly affected.

IT is completely responsible for how organized our civilization has become. The corporate world was only made possible by the communication information technology has put in place between both computer software and hardware. From a personal stand point, it would be difficult for most people to name a single person doesn't use the internet on a regular basis.

With the increasing new technologies coming out everyday, employees in the Information Technology work force must constantly re-educate themselves with all the new technologies. This makes IT a very demanding field as it is always developing and perfecting. The process of improvement is what makes this such a desirable aspect to almost any business. It is very important for anyone in the IT field to always stay up to date with all newly developing technologies that relate to their industry. IT is now the complete backbone to almost any business and its ability to be competitive and efficient.

The broad subject concerned with all aspects of managing and processing information, especially within a large organization or company. Because computers are central to information management, computer departments within companies and universities are often called IT departments. Some companies refer to this department as IS (Information Services) or MIS (Management Information Services).

The penguin dictionary of computers defines it as "a portmanteau phrase to cover all aspects of the art or science of processing data to produce information". It includes computer software, hardware, programs, and databases, semiconductor chips that put together process and produce the output.

Output can be expressed in human readable form (printouts) or in machine readable form (series of electronic pulses) which are further used to control a any other machine, tool or device. Information technology also includes networking of computers and databases exchanging and feeding information between one another.

Basic understanding of and about technology law warrants proper grasp and appreciation about technology itself. Inherently technology law, like any other emerging facts of law, is purely inter-disciplinary in nature. Hence, it is now proposed to explain and introduce some of essential and relevant aspects of information technology.

Importance of information technology

The importance of information technology cannot be ignored by banking and insurance sectors, except at the cost of elimination from the competition. This is so because the use of information technology produces certain advantages, which are not available when the traditional and conventional methods of doing business are used. The use of information technology generates the following advantages and benefits:

- easy handling of day to day affairs of an organization,
- speedy disposal of routine and daily works,
- assurance of authenticity, integrity and confidentiality in the functioning of the organization,

- cost economy,

- integration and interaction with the global institutions and organizations,

- better communication and presentation facilities,

- assurance of safety and sound security of the sensitive and valuable information, like trade secrets,

- instant transfer of data and information where the situation demands,

- it provides access to public documents which are digitalized by various department s of the Government,

- for making online payments of various bills and dues,

- to file statutory documents online , etc.

These benefits development of information technology can be claimed by all business ventures, including banking and insurance sectors, but apart from that its advantages are claimed by various other sectors which are discussed as follow :

1. Development to Banking business,

2. Development in Forensic Science and Police Wireless

3. Development in Railways

4. Development of IT in Agriculture

5. Role of Information Technology in Alternative Dispute Redressal & Judicial recognition

6. Development of IT in Health and Medicine

1) Development to Banking business

The benefits and advantages of information technology for the smooth and efficient functioning of the banking business cannot be disregarded and sidelined. This is more so when a bank proposes to deal in "Internet banking " which is an important offshoot of information technology. Its proper and methodical use can bring the following advantages.

(A) Sound Payment System:

The usage of electronic means of funds movement and settlement is still in its stages of formative years. The various forms of electronic based payment, such as credit cards, Automated Teller Machines (ATMs),

Stored Value cards, Shared Payment Network Service (SPNS) etc, are emerging at an incredible speed. Many banks have made initiatives aimed at electronic modes of funds movement.

While this is a positive development, it needs to be ensured that such funds transfers are made in a high level of security so that no unauthorized usage occurs in the newer modes being implemented by banks. It is this area, which has been the focus of attention by the Reserve Bank - and the efforts have now resulted in the form of the Structured Financial Messaging Solution (SFMS).

The SFMS incorporates adequate security measures, including that of Public Key Infrastructure (PKI), with encryption software equivalent to some of the best security measure in the world. The use of the SFMS over the INFINET would automatically provide safe, secure and efficient funds transfers with the added benefit of the settlement of inter-bank funds transfers taking place in the books of account of banks, maintained with the Reserve Bank, thereby providing for finality of the settlement.

Further, the message formats used in SFMS are very similar to those used by SWIFT, resulting in ease of usage by the banking community in the country. This secure messaging backbone can be used for a number of intra-bank applications also.

(B) Effective Currency Management

The impact of technology on the issuances of Bank Notes and Currency Management by Central bank is apparent. The technology offers us immense opportunities to significantly improve our performance of this core function. Given the high value and volume of currency in circulation, the vast geographic spread of currency operations, the largest distribution channel for the supply of currency, prevalent marked preference for cash and currency handling practices, currency management in India is a challenging and strenuous task.

In 1999, the Reserve Bank of India announced a "Clean Note Policy" to bring about improvements of the quality of notes in circulation and technology has played an indispensable role in enabling the Bank to provide better quality notes to the general public. The information technology makes the task of currency management easy, effective, economical and speedier.

2) Development in Forensic Science and Police Wireless

The modernization and manpower development of Information Technology in the Central Forensic Science Laboratories and GEQDs, which were started in the Seventh Plan, has had an immense development .

The research areas envisaged pertain DNA finger printing; cadaver entomology; immuno-assay techniques; classification of handwriting characteristics; instrumental techniques for examining writing materials; computerized image processing of firearms and ammunition; development of computerized system for superimposition; immuno diagnostic technique, hair identification, range and time of firing and explosive analysis, etc.

It is thus expected that rapidity and sophistication would be introduced by way of video- fit techniques, laser-tracing, holography, image processing, computer aided automatic finger print identification system and initiatives taken in new frontier areas like forensic psychology. Suitable structure and mechanism would be evolved for the formulation, implementation and monitoring of S&T schemes under the Forensic Science.

In the area of police wireless, the main thrust has been to achieve communication link from the national capital up to rural police station through State Headquarters, Range Headquarters, and District Headquarters. This is proposed to be achieved through the development of high speed message switch, micro processor based specifically designed computerized connectors, pocket radio system, micro earth station and secrecy devices and multi-access radio telephone.

3) Development in Railways

Indian Railways is one of the largest systems in the world. It is said that information technology (IT), which is being introduced into various fields, is a key to the development in the 21st century. Technology innovative provider of the In Rule(TM) business rules engine for automating application decision logic that involves rules, calculations and dynamic user interfaces, today announced the expansion of its partner network in response to the needs of its growing customer base.

The development of information and technology shows that safety, efficiency and convenience have been improved in the areas of railway use, operations and maintenance.

This is followed by a section on a new train control system for high-density lines that uses methods for transmitting information to the train about the distance to the position at which the train must stop, which is necessary for train control. This system is realized through the advanced application of information technology.

Until now, it has been impossible to realize efficient operations in high-density lines due to limitations of existing signal technology. Further information technology has been used for train operation, security and ticket booking/issuing systems, must more actively apply information technology to improve safety, comfort and convenience.

Therefore, we are committing research and development to prevent accidents and dramatically improve passenger services by utilizing information technology to the maximum extent, to the Railway Technical Research Institute (RTRI). As a means to introduce information technology into various fields of transport service, we are promoting researches to construct a "Comprehensive Transport Information Providing System." and will continue to implement the policies to utilize information technology.

4) Development of IT in Agriculture

Agriculture is the backbone of the Indian economy. It accounts for 27% of GDP, contributes 21% of total exports, and raw materials to several industries. About two third of Indian population depends on the agricultural sector for their means of livelihood. Therefore IT has a major role to play in all facets of Indian agriculture.

In addition to facilitating farmers in improving the efficiency and productivity of agriculture and allied activities, the potential of IT lies in bringing about an overall qualitative improvement in life by providing timely and quality information inputs for decision making.

The personnel who work for the welfare of Indian farmers, such as extension workers, do not have access to latest information which hinders their ability to serve the farming community effectively. In the context nonagricultural, the potential of IT can be assessed broadly under two heads:

a) as a tool for direct contribution to agricultural productivity

b) as an indirect tool for empowering farmers to take informed and quality decisions which will have positive impact on the way agriculture and allied activities are conducted.

5) Role of Information Technology in Alternative Dispute Redersal and Judicial Recognition

Information technology provides opportunities to facilitate communication and so assist in prevention and management of disputes. ADR services can use information technology to provide information to parties in case of disputes arise between the parties and also to complement and substitute for, traditional information system. Information technology can also play a valuable role in supporting the quality of ADR practice through more effective supervision, assessment, training, information management, research and evaluation.

The Role of Information Technology in Business

The role of information technology systems in a business environment can be classified into four broad categories. These categories include function performance, communication through networking, management and enterprise roles.

Information technology provides commercial and industrial systems for businesses. These systems enable businesses to function effectively and efficiently.

Function IT Systems

Function IT systems are applications that allow individuals to function effectively in the workplace. Examples of common IT systems that enhance workplace functions are word processor applications, spreadsheet applications, statistical analysis software and computer aided design (CAD) programs. Employees can work and perform their task individually or collectively using these specialized software technologies.

Network IT Systems

Network IT systems allow effective communication within and outside an organisation. Examples range from simple e-mail (electronic mail) to blogs, wiki sites, IM (instant messaging) and electronic conferencing systems. These types of technologies promote interaction and collaboration among working groups and also facilitate quick information flow at all levels.

Management IT systems

Management IT systems(MITS) can be defined as planned applications that are designed to process data and transform the processed data into useful information for management decision making.

It should be noted that Management Information systems (MIS) are subsets of Enterprise IT systems (this is explained later on in this article). However, because of the vital role MIS play in a business environment, it is considered here as a major information technology for businesses.

In a typical scenario, management operates at different levels and so it is possible to apply management information systems at these varied levels.

Basic examples of management information systems are human resources management systems, financial management information systems and marketing management information systems.

Enterprise IT Systems

Enterprise IT systems are technologies designed to integrate and manage entire business processes for large organisations. Typically, enterprise application software is hosted on large servers over a computer network. Transmission of information can either be internal or external.

Examples of enterprise information systems may be accounting software, health care specific software or Electronic Data Interchange (EDI). Another good example of software application within this category is Customer relationship management software (CRM).

The role of Information technology in business is wide and varied. It can be said that IT provides a huge range of capabilities that enhance management performance at all levels. It is therefore important to understand the four major categories of IT systems and their functions and roles in a business environment.

Technology is rapidly changing the way that businesses communicate and function every day. It is important for managers to take a proactive role in understanding emerging technology trends and how they may affect a company's business model by investing in an ongoing program of information technology training for all levels of staff. Management training in particular is essential for ensuring the right technologies are pursued to ensure business success. Viewing technology as a direct influencer on the business as a whole ensures consistent alignment of goals throughout the enterprise.

Career In IT - Time To Get Into The IT Industry

Information technology relates to the management aspect and application of information together with its processing using various tools. All sectors today are directly dependent on technology and information systems, and this are among the reasons why a career in IT today delivers better opportunities for job seekers.

An individual from any field can seek an IT career because computers and networks have become integral part and parcels of our lives, and graduates from other disciplines can kick start their IT career by getting their skills polished by obtaining proper IT related certifications.

IT careers that are related to software programming require strong technical knowledge on the operation of various programming languages such as.Net, Java, C++, Oracle, Ruby & Rails among others whereas to become better acquainted with the hardware part of it, you have to be good in digital electronics and have the ability to troubleshoot various electronic components.

Information technology applications is today incredibly dynamic and it has managed to establish footprints in various sectors such as in banking, medicine, transport, agriculture, and law among others. Organizations that develop these technologies have also been lauded for their efforts to nurture new careers such as Network professionals and mobile applications developer, and the high salary being paid out to these individuals has been cited as to the main reason as to why these careers continue to flourish.

IT industry related career courses are available at various levels from different institutions. This particular industry offers career opportunities to non technical personnel as well. Due to the IT industry nature of constant innovation, this has managed to inject an impetus to a number of IT careers with recent results depicting that IT related professions are going to flourish for a very long period of time.

Because of commitments and sound strategic policies from technological companies, the IT industry has become so successful and has already left a mark in various sectors.

High Paying Jobs in the Field of Information Technology

There are wide range of high paying jobs in the field of Information Technology. Getting a high paying job is easy today, but doing the required justice to such Jobs is a challenging part.The most important thing for being qualified for the Job is Knowledge and Communication skills. In some of the high paying jobs like Database Administrators, Network Administrator, Developers, it is important for an employee to be available at service any time 24x7 round the clock which is one of the important responsibility for such jobs.

Education is one key to a good job. In today's job market what you know determines what you earn. The more you know the more you make. When a Job seeker is confident about his knowledge, attitude, hard work and team spirit, it yields him success in all of the attempts he makes. Many companies look forward to the candidates with such attitude and commitments at high posts where results matter more than the efforts.

Getting a Job Interview is very easy but carrying it out further through the process of recruitment and finally getting selected is all dependent on individuals knowledge, qualification, approach, presentation, winning the hearts of the interviewer by smarter answers etc... Thus one should always be prepared in every aspects of the interview which is one of the useful tips in getting the different Jobs with ease. Preparing self for the best interview is the key here.

Other important key to get the Jobs is presenting yourself in an interview both professionally and physical appearance. Many a times it is important for an individual to carry his appearance, attire and behavior to match it with the qualification and knowledge he owns. It is one of the most important factors which many individual ignore to take care of but is a very decisive factor in any interview today. As we all know that "How you look tells about how you manage yourself". Thus unless we manage .

CHAPTER 2

C SHARP (C#)

To start at the very beginning, C# is a modern language created by Microsoft as part of its .NET platform of languages. .NET is a layer of software that makes it easier for you to write programs that can communicate with the operating system (in this case, Windows). As the name implies, C# has its roots in C++, but over three versions, it has evolved its own techniques and elements that make it distinct. Most important, C# has the backing of the .NET Framework behind it, which we'll get into shortly.

We're not going to assume that you have any C++ experience, so we won't frame our discussions of C# in terms of C++, or any other programming language. What you need to know right now is that you can write applications in C# that will do just about anything you need to do.

You can write applications to manage your company's inventory (interacting with a database); you can write applications to analyze documents; you can write games; you can create an entire operating system in C# if you have a mind to.

The .NET Framework allows C# to operate seamlessly with Windows, and take advantage of the familiar Windows features that users all over the world already know. You can also create C# applications that you can use on the Web, in much the same way.

To be completely honest, most modern object-oriented languages are rather similar underneath. The choice of one over the other is usually just a matter of personal preference. C# and Visual Basic have the advantage of the .NET Framework, but third-party languages can interact with the framework, too.

C#'s similarity to C++ and Java makes it easy to learn for programmers familiar with those languages, but it's also easy to learn as your first language. Once you have the basics of C# down, you'll find it much easier to learn any other language you want to.

What is C#?

C#, as mentioned earlier, is one of the languages you can use to create applications that will run in the .NET CLR. It is an evolution of the C and C++ languages and has been created by Microsoft specifically to work with the .NET platform. The C# language has been designed to incorporate many of the best features from other languages, while clearing up their problems.

Developing applications using C# is simpler than using C++, because the language syntax is simpler. Still, C# is a powerful language, and there is little you might want to do in C++ that you can't do in C#. Having said that, those features of C# that parallel the more advanced features of C++, such as directly accessing and manipulating system memory, can be carried out only by using code marked as unsafe.

This advanced programmatic technique is potentially dangerous (hence its name) because it is possible to overwrite system-critical blocks of memory with potentially catastrophic results. For this reason, and others, this book does not cover that topic.

At times, C# code is slightly more verbose than C++. This is a consequence of C# being a type-safe language (unlike C++). In layperson's terms, this means that once some data has been assigned to a type, it cannot subsequently transform itself into another unrelated type. Consequently, strict rules must be adhered to when converting between types, which means you will often need to write more code to carry out the same task in C# than you might write in C++.

However, you get two benefits: the code is more robust and debugging is simpler, and .NET can always track the type of a piece of data at any time. In C#, you therefore may not be able to do things such as ?take the region of memory 4 bytes into this data and 10 bytes long and interpret it as X,? but that's not necessarily a bad thing.

C# is just one of the languages available for .NET development, but it is certainly the best. It has the advantage of being the only language designed from the ground up for the .NET Framework and is the principal language used in versions of .NET that are ported to other operating systems.

To keep languages such as the .NET version of Visual Basic as similar as possible to their predecessors yet compliant with the CLR, certain features of the .NET code library are not fully supported, or at least require unusual syntax. By contrast, C# can make use of every feature that the .NET Framework code library has to offer. The latest version of .NET includes several additions to the C# language, partly in response to requests from developers, making it even more powerful.

Applications You Can Write with C#

The .NET Framework has no restrictions on the types of applications that are possible, as discussed earlier. C# uses the framework and therefore has no restrictions on possible applications. However, here are a few of the more common application types:

Windows applications-Applications, such as Microsoft Office, that have a familiar Windows look and feel about them. This is made simple by using the Windows Forms module of the .NET Framework, which is a library of controls (such as buttons, toolbars, menus, and so on) that you can use to build a Windows user interface (UI). Alternatively, you can use Windows Presentation Foundation (WPF) to build Windows applications, which gives you much greater flexibility and power.

Web applications-Web pages such as those that might be viewed through any Web browser. The .NET Framework includes a powerful system for generating Web content dynamically, enabling personalization, security, and much more. This system is called ASP.NET (Active Server Pages .NET), and you can use C# to create ASP.NET applications using Web Forms. You can also write applications that run inside the browser with Silverlight.

Web services-An exciting way to create versatile distributed applications. Using Web services you can exchange virtually any data over the Internet, using the same simple syntax regardless of the language used to create a Web service or the system on which it resides. For more advanced capabilities, you can also create Windows Communication Foundation (WCF) services.

Any of these types may also require some form of database access, which can be achieved using the ADO.NET (Active Data Objects .NET) section of the .NET Framework, through the ADO.NET Entity Framework, or through the LINQ (Language Integrated Query) capabilities of C#. Many other resources can be drawn on, such as tools for creating networking components, outputting graphics, performing complex mathematical tasks, and so on.

What is the difference between C, C++ and C#?

As C is the base of C++ and C# which means they must be having some advantage over C but still C is used in many places.

And is there any difference in C and C++ other than OOP.

It helps to think of programming languages in terms of how closely they are able to control what a computer is actually doing. These are commonly classified as low-, intermediate- and high-level programming languages. Computers execute machine code, and assembly language is considered the lowest level programming language; it is a human readable version of machine code.

C was created to provide a structural programming language that is easier to use than assembly. It is considered a low-level programming language with little to no loss in performance relative to assembly. This made C the natural choice for building operating systems and low-level software on computers because it allowed for easier development at near-assembly performance.

C++ is essentially an extension of C. The original C++ compilers just pre-compiled directly into C, which was then compiled to machine code, while modern C++ compilers can easily compile C or C++ into machine code. C++ was designed to allow developers to use all of the existing features of C but provides a number of extensions to support object-oriented programming techniques in an intermediate-level programming language.

C# is a complete outlier in this list. Despite it's name, it has far more in common with Java than C or C++. C# is an object-oriented, high-level programming language. Like Java, C# provides a number of features to make it easier for a developer to code in this language such as type checking, bounds checking, uninitialized variable checking, and garbage collection. While the language does not technically specify how it is executed, C# is most commonly compiled into byte-code (rather than machine code) and executes on a virtual machine (like Java) that converts the application into machine code on the fly.

Developers who are focused on performance still pick C or C++ as their language of choice. Nearly all operating systems (kernel and low-level system software) are written in C, C++ or some combination of the two. Most high-profile server and desktop software is also written in C++. For example, most web browsers, office suites and games are written in C or C++. C# remains a common choice for internal/enterprise applications but is less common for commercial software.

Contrary to the way it looks, C is what I'd call an "expression-oriented" language, with some imperative and (minimally) declarative elements layered on top. Imperative elements govern control flow.

Expression elements mostly deal with computation, though the ?: operator governs control flow, along with giving a result. Structs/unions, along with bitfields, are a declarative feature that allow the programmer to create offsets inside a defined area of memory, and/or create types which allow the program to allocate more areas of memory, which can be navigated by offsets.

C++ layers declarative syntax on top of the aforementioned features of C, to define an extra layer of scope for functions, with parameterized typing, called "classes." It greatly expands upon the concept of the struct in C, by attaching strong typing to functions (the types of which can be parameterized), and heap allocations (which can also be parameterized), and adding an implied "this" pointer to functions that are associated with structured data. Other features include:

A table of pointers inside of these expanded structs, which may exist inside of heap allocations, to functions that are defined in derived classes, to enable "downward" polymorphism, when functions associated with structured data are called.

A new type of reference called an "alias." I might call it a "roving variable." Like a pointer, it can be made to reference different areas of memory, but like a variable, it can be used to assign rvalues of its type to memory locations without the need to explicitly dereference it. An alias doesn't function like a variable by itself. It needs a defined address space (a declared variable, or defined structure of some sort, that is known to it) in order to function as a variable.

A designator called "const" that allows values to be assigned to variables once, but not modified.

A meta-structural feature called "templates" that allows types to be parameterized (these types are filled in when the source is compiled).

A little bit of meta-programming, where during run-time some information can become known about the type of an object.

Lambdas were recently added to C++. From what I understand, these are functions that are defined inline, and use an abbreviated syntax.

Like with C, C++ takes a layered approach to these different aspects. As a result, C++ does not necessarily warn you if you do something like an assignment inside of a conditional test expression.

C# adopted some syntactic features of C++, but it doesn't compile and run the way C++ does. C# holds your hand more than C++ does. It doesn't allow certain expressions to be used inside of certain constructs (like an assignment inside a test condition), as some things are considered bad form, and probably a mistake.

Like with C++, what C# calls classes are an expansion on the struct concept from C, but there are no pointers in C# code, unless you explicitly go into "native" mode. I forget how this is done, but it is possible to go down to the machine level, inside a "confined" space, inside a C# program. The runtime keeps the pointers, and hands references to them to the running code. This is to enable garbage collection, which C++ doesn't have.

A consequence of this is that deallocating memory is explicitly deterministic in C++, but it's not in C#. Memory is made available for garbage collection in

C# when a variable no longer refers to a value or object, but when that memory is deallocated and cleared is determined by the runtime. In C++, memory can only be deallocated explicitly, using a "delete" command.

C# has two types of variables: "value" and "object." Variables of object type are stored on the heap. Value type variables are not. Value type variables behave rather like "native" variables in C++ (types like "int"), except that they are classes, and the values that are assigned to them are classes or structs. The way you can tell the difference between the two is that value type variables can take a literal. You can say:int a = 10;

Variables of object type have to receive an object that was brought into existence by the "new" operator, which allocates the object on the heap. This behavior will be familiar to C++ programmers.

It is possible to convert between the two types of variables, doing what's called "boxing" and "unboxing." In C++ this would be accomplished through explicit or implicit cast operators.

Variables of object type function rather like aliases in C++, except they don't need a defined address space. They just refer to objects in memory (or null, if they refer to nothing). There is some "magic" under the covers about how the runtime stores these values, and arrives at the stored values (when retrieving them), since again, there are no pointers. Objects are just bound to object variables.

The programmer is not supposed to concern themselves with how. There is no relationship between a variable of object type and where an object is stored in memory. To make another analogy, object variables function rather like keys in a hash table, referring to objects that are stored along with the keys.

Object variables can be re-assigned to different pieces of memory by reassigning them to different objects, though the runtime arranges what memory is accessed. The programmer has no explicit control over that. All the programmer knows is that a variable may be referencing something else when s/he reassigns a variable to another object.

Similar to C++, in C# you define functions that are associated with structured data, though unlike C++, you cannot define free-standing functions that are not associated with a class.

C# implements the same basic polymorphic function logic within objects as C++ does, though how it does it I don't think is made known to programmers.

Generics were eventually added to the language, which are analogous to templates in C++. They allow types to be parameterized.

C# has lambdas, like C++'s recent addition of lambdas. Before .Net got lambdas, Microsoft introduced anonymous functions, which functioned like lambdas, but were more verbose, and were generally used to handle event logic.

In more recent versions of C#, it has been possible to extend class definitions, so that programmers who use a framework can add methods to an existing class without having to create a derived class, modifying the original source code, or recompiling it. C++ has not had this capability.

C# modules (DLLs) can be called up by version number. I haven't heard of any implementation of C++ that has that capability.

C# modules can be incrementally downloaded over the internet and late-bound into a running program, as needed. C/C++ hasn't had that ability in their runtimes, except via. binary DLLs in Windows, or .so libraries in Unix (or some equivalent on Linux). In C/C++ it's done through OS calls. In .Net it's done through calls to the Framework's library.

From what I've understood, C has been more portable between platforms than C++ (though perhaps this has improved since I last used C++, which was in 2006). C# doesn't have much portability. If you want to use the most up-to-date version of C#, you have to use it on a version of

Windows (with one exception, which I talk about below).

If you're able to skimp on the version, there is an open source implementation of the .Net runtime called Mono that runs on multiple platforms, with its own C# compiler. It is able to emulate Windows GUI functions in client apps.

The following table contains important comparisons between C++ and C# features. If you are a C++ programmer, this table will give you the most important differences between the two languages at a glance. For details, use the link to browse to the detailed topic.

Comparison Between C++ and C#

Let's start with the common points: all three of them (four of them, if we add Java) use the same principles in syntax: the C way.

C was first, and a history of C will make you understand why C is important. C, however, in its goal to become a portable assembler (a common sense common subset) had other priorities, and wanted to be as close to the metal as possible.

C++ includes all that C has, and adds to that encapsulation, polymorphism, templates and a whole standard library based on templates. Using data containers becomes much easier. The differences between C and C++ are subtle - where you could just assign a void * to a char *, for example, you have to do a proper cast; type checking is more strict in C++. But other than that, C++ is just a cleaner version of C, with OOP and metaprogramming added.

C# and Java discard C for C++. They take C++, throw away the pointer notation, and all variables become hidden pointers (except for the value types, primitive types, due to performance reasons). They add forcibly garbage collection, metadata to your classes, all the objects will be derived from a base class, called object or Object, which adds automatically virtual methods to objects, and they never compile to native code; instead they compile to an evolved machine language called IL for C# and bytecode for Java.

This makes them require an interpreter to run said code, and transform it in native code, or just interpret the code and run it like a Virtual Machine. Since probably that was the initial approach, Java's interpreter is called JVM (Java Virtual Machine), while C#'s is called CLR (Common Language Runtime). But in the end, to obtain performance, the interpreters try to actually generate native code, so they all come with a translator of intermediary code to native code. This is the so-called JIT (Just In Time) compilation.

But the interpreted code is a performance issue, and the supporters for the languages create new ways to improve said performance. For example, Microsoft chose to actually run the JIT before even loading some modules, only one time, so when the .NET framework gets an update, you'll see some processes busy for a long time: they will transform your common language code to native code before you even use them, and store a cached version to be available for all programs.

The difference between C#/Java and C is too big, but the differences between C#/Java and C++ are easier to pick and the most important, other than said updates to the language, are the adoption of a pure OOP approach to programming. C# does it less than Java, but Java has these purists that for a lot of time refused to do things non-OOP (and that is usually bad, because OOP is just one paradigm, but it cannot cover everything without huge performance issues).

C# and Java are also 'owned' languages. If you choose C#, you are tied to Microsoft products (although Mono lives on a developers promise from Microsoft and the fact that C# is defined as an ECMA standard). Microsoft drives the language, as well as the .NET framework that actually gives value to C# as a language.

Java used to be owned by Sun, which now has been taken over by Oracle. I won't say more, but as we speak, Oracle has some long standing lawsuit against

Google for using Java 'not how we wanted you to use it'. So there's a word of warning there, as well as the fact that Oracle won't be able to drive a language the same way Microsoft does. And C# is really ages ahead of Java.

In the mean time, C++ has this C++11 extension. This extension, and the coming C++14, aims to improve the language, to make it more of a modern language. You can see new smart-pointers, lambdas support, ranged loops and all sort of improvements for the developer that also keep the overhead of not using them to 0. C++ always had this don't pay for what you don't use approach, that makes it a more mature language.

C is a great language, gnu C is probably the greatest language of all time. The reason is that it is both very low level, and yet it has no barriers to scaling up to making arbitrarily complicated projects. It is the only language that a former assembly programmer can program in without tearing the hair out. Perl is a close runner up here, but the hair (slowly) comes out. With other languages, you're bald.

There is a fundamental principle in C that is not respected in any other language: complete binary data transparency. in C, you know exactly what you get with your data. That means if you say "struct froo {int i;double x; char c;}. you know exactly what you are getting in memory, byte by byte, even usually in what order.

The stuff that isn't specified in the standard is often standardized by the compiler anyway, and on non-aligned architectures like Intel, it's exactly what you think it is--- an int, followed by a double, followed by a char, exactly 15 bytes long. No type modifier, no added information, like a UNIX file, it's just clean data exactly like what you wanted.

It will place consecutive data consecutive in memory. Stuff you allocate in a function gets allocated on the stack exactly as you declare it (usually in the same order), stuff you allocate with malloc goes on the heap exactly where you think it is (the information about the page allocation is slightly behind the data in Linux if I remember right).

The memory layout of all your data is under your control, and there are no compiler generated surprises, because the compiler hardly does anything, and it doesn't do anything without you asking for it specifically. C also can compile lightning fast, if you don't use C++, it was compiling on 1970s hardware, and it has a preprocessor that's faster than cat.

The algorithms are also transparent, you can see more or less exactly what machine code will get emitted from your instructions. Here C is not completely ideal, because its expressions are modelled on previous high level languages, and so it is lacking three things that it really should have had:

1. a primitive swap--- you can't primitively swap the value in a with the value in b.

2. carry sensitivity--- you can't talk about the carry on an add, it's unspeakable.

3. high-bits of multiplication--- you can't talk about the high 32 or 64 bits of a times b, also unspeakable.

The ANSI standard included one useless thing that makes writing an ANSI compiler hell: named bitfields. Those are so useless, everyone uses masks, and they get turned into masks anyway, and still these stupid bit-fields wreck any cheap and quick ANSI compiler. I hope tcc (the tiny c compiler) avoids implementing bit-fields, but they are striving for ANSI compatibility.

All of these are there in the architecture, and are available to an assembly programmer. Gcc will figure out when you are swapping often and put in a swap, but if you want to implement a bigint, you need assembly, because you can't access the carry or the high bits from C. This is the only intolerable annoyance left in C for the assembly programmer.

Aside from these three annoyances, anything else you do in assembly you can do in C. I am assuming you are using gnu C, which includes computed goto, named enum, named initializer, nested functions, and all the other gnu extensions which should have been in the ANSI standards to begin with, but weren't (some of them are there now). Gnu C also has a named return value extension which doesn't work in C, but should.

C also doesn't stop you from doing tsk, tsk, naughty things. You can get a pointer to your own code, and rewrite your program's machine code (with appropriate system calls). You can allocate a block of code and emit machine code into it, and jump to this code. You can "goto" anywhere you want. You can wreck your own stack. You can access all the operating-system allocated information about the pages of memory you are writing to.

And if insist that you really want to fiddle with the registers, you can, because you can embed assembly anytime. You can also control the register allocation in gcc, you can micromanage the compiler as far as you like.This made C the superstar of languages, because it really understood what assembly programmers wanted. Since it could be used to write an operating system, it replaced assembly programming in the 1980s, and this is probably irreversible, even though the major motivation, lack of a standard architecture, is now moot, because Intel architecture is standard today.

C++ took C and added object orientation. Some of C++ is harmless and nice, like // comments, structs with automatic typedef, default values functions, and namespaces (which really help keep the code separate and modular). Even making structs include functions is no big deal, it does make the code a little prettier.

But C++ became C++ rather than a dialect of C when it went on to break the commandment: thou shalt keep the data binary transparent, It broke it in such a seemingly harmless looking way, though, that Stroustroup probably said "What's the big deal?"

The culprit was the virtual function table. There are two kinds of classes in C++, the ones that are virtual and the ones that are not. If you don't use any virtual functions, you might as well be using a really annoyingly nitpicky C. But when you declare functions virtual, then you get a non-transparent change in your data structure.

At the beginning of every instance of your structure you get a pointer, and this pointer points to a virtual function table, and this virtual function table has a list of pointers to all the functions you declared virtual, which are the ones that get called when you try to call the function of this name on the given data type.

When a class inherits from your class, it gets a copy of your virtual function table, and it can override the virtual functions and redeclare them. Then the pointers in the function table are overwritten. This is all done by the compiler, at compile time, by arranging the virtual function table, and that's nice. But it is not nice in one way: the data is there and is inaccessible by the program! Commandment broken.

What does this mean? It means that suppose you declare a class of "number types", which makes virtual addition. Then when you declare a quaternion to be (number_type A,B,C,D), you get four number-type objects, which contain a virtual function table pointer each.

That's 8 bytes of function table pointer + 1 byte data. Overall, 4 bytes data, 32 bytes of function pointers! And it's stupid--- you know for sure that the four objects are all the same number-type, but because the virtual function table is welded onto the data-type, you can't separate it out. Breaking the commandment comes back to byte you.

This means that C++ is useless for designing a number class which can generate efficient codes for various mathematical objects, you still need to roll your own. If you do write a general thing, it has to be a template, and this is itself a nightmare that C++ introduces to get around these limitations.

If you use standard C++ for these cheap things, the quaternion multiplication becomes horribly inefficient, and you might as well be using a high level language.

The other problem is that you aren't allowed to modify the virtual function table at runtime, it's hard wired by the compiler. This means if you decide you want to change the way a particular class should do x or y, you can't overwrite the function table pointer, it's not accessible to you. You can hack it up in gcc, it is possible, but it is hard because the language is violating the data transparancy commandment.

This feature is what Java and C# add. They make it that you can construct classes and modify them whenever you like, at runtime. But they are never low level, because as much as they promise compilation to machine code, it's never going to happen, it was just hype. So they stay useless for high performance scientific computing, which is always at the machine limits. They also violate the commandment much more freely, so that you can't even use dirty pointers.

CHAPTER 3

ADVANTAGE OF C# OVER C PROGRAMMING AND C++

C# is just a language targeting CLR. thus,I think the advantages mainly result from .net framework.

I have little knowledge of Java, but compared with C++. C# has the following features:

1. C# is pure object-oriented,but C++ is a mixture of object-oriented and procedure-oriented.

2. C# is more type safe

3. you need not put much attention on such problems as memory leak, which is troubling problem for C++ programmer.

4. The Assembly concept solves the versioning control problem well.

5.Ease-to-development, The rich class library makes many functions easy to be implemented.

6.Cross-platform. you application will run well only if the machine installed the .NET framework.

7.Good support for distributed system.

There are much more features, you can experience during development. However, each language has its advantage, you can select language depending on you application.

The main advantage of C# is that it runs on the CLR, making it easy to integrate with components written in other languages (specifically, CLR-compatible languages) and many of Microsoft's proprietary technologies. Also note that much of .NET has been standardized, which means that it could run on other platforms (google the mono project for more info), but this isn't well-supported.

Writing in C# also gives one access to all the .NET Framework class libraries, which are quite extensive. While these libraries might support specific features better than in Java (WPF is arguably better suited for rich multimedia GUIs than java.swing), on the whole Java SDK's feature set if very similar to the .NET

Framework and one can't say one is better than the other in general.

C# has many language constructs that java lacks, such as delegates (function pointers) and operator overloading. However, Java has its own way of solving the same kinds of problems that these feature address, and while the subject is often hotly debated, there is really no way to objectively determine which approach is "better." However, I think most would agree that C#'s support for generics is more robust than Java's. On the other hand, Java's enums are far more robust than C#'s.

C# 3.0 will bring a lot of new language features, including extension methods, lamda expressions, and query expressions. For me, this is a big win for C#.

Also, the designers of the .NET Framework and C# did a good job thinking about the developer's needs. The tool support for .NET is overall very good, and it is obvious from the design of the libraries that the designer's spent a lot of time thinking about the learning curve and ease-of-use from the developer's standpoint.

C# is better than C++ in that:

- It has native garbage-collection.
- It allows you to treat class-methods' signatures as free functions (i.e. ignoring the statically typed this pointer argument), and hence create more dynamic and flexible relationships between classes. edit if you don't know what this means, then try assigning a member method returning void and accepting void to a void (*ptr)() variable. C# delegates carry the this pointer with them, but the user doesn't always have to care about that. They can just assign a void() method of any class to any other void() delegate.
- It has a huge standard library with so much useful stuff that's well-implemented and easy to use.
- It allows for both managed and native code blocks.

Assembly versioning easily remedy DLL hell problems.

You can set classes, methods and fields to be assembly-internal (which means they are accessible from anywhere within the DLL they're declared in, but not from other assemblies).

C# is better than Java in that:

Instead of a lot of noise (EJB, private static class implementations, etc) you get elegant and friendly native constructs such as Properties and Events.

You have real generics (not the bad casting joke that Java calls generics), and you can perform reflection on them.

- It supports native resource-management idioms (the using statement). Java 7 is also going to support this, but C# has had it for a way longer time.
- It doesn't have checked exceptions :) (debatable whether this is good or bad)

- It's deeply integrated with Windows, if that's what you want.

- It has Lambdas and LINQ, therefore supporting a small amount of functional programming.

- It allows for both generic covariance and contravariance explicitly.

- It has dynamic variables, if you want them.

- Better enumeration support, with the yield statement.

- It allows you to define new value (or non-reference) types.

Java doesn't have it (you have to explicitly do a try/finally). C++ has auto pointers which are great for RAII, and (if you know what you're doing) can also substitute garbage-collection.

For example if you need to access a field by a this pointer, and bind the method that does it to a generic function pointer (i.e. not in the same class), then there's simply no native way to do it. In C#, you get the for free. You don't even have to know how it works.

By "treating member methods as free functions" I meant that you can't, for example, natively bind a member method to a free function signature, because the member method "secretly" needs the this pointer.

The using statement, obviously along with IDisposable wrappers, is a great example of RAII. See this link. Consider that you don't need RAII as much in C# as you do in C++, because you have the GC. For the specific times you do need it, you can explicitly use the using statement.

Another little reminder: freeing memory is an expensive procedure. GC have their performance advantage in a lot of cases (especially when you have lots of memory). Memory won't get leaked, and you won't be spending a lot of time on deallocating. What's more, allocation is faster as well, since you don't allocate memory every time, only once in a while. Calling new is simply incrementing a last-object-pointer.

"C# is worse in that it has garbage collection". This is indeed subjective, but as I stated at the top, for most modern, typical application development, garbage collection is one hell of an advantage.

In C++, your choices are either to manually manage your memory using new and delete, which empirically always leads to errors here and there, or (with C++11) you can use auto pointers natively, but keep in mind that they add lots and lots of noise to the code. So GC still has an edge there.

"Generics are way weaker than templates" - I just don't know where you got that from. Templates might have their advantages, but in my experience constraints, generic parameter type-checking, contravariance and covariance are much stronger and elegant tools. The strength in templates is that they let you play with the language a bit, which might be cool, but also causes lots of headaches when you want to debug something.

The Environment

.NET Framework and Windows clients

Windows is the dominating Operating System on client computers. The best GUI frameworks for Windows applications is Winforms and WPF together with .NET Framework. The best programming language to work with the .NET Framework and it's APIs is C#. Java is not an alternative for this. And C++ is an older language without automatic memory management.

C# is similar to C++ but has automatic memory management and you don't have to work with pointers, which make you more productive. C++ can still be the best option for some cases, but not for form-intensive database applications that is common in business.

IIS and Windows Server

If you are used to work in the Windows environment and with C#, you will need the least investment to learn IIS for server programming and Windows Server for basic administration.

Active Directory and Windows Server

If you are developing software that is going to be deployed in company networks, it's likely that they use an Windows centered environment using a Windows Server with Active Directory. In such an environment it's easist to integrate and deploy an solution made in C# and .NET Framework.

Yes, C# is a better language with more modern features than C++ and Java, but that is not the most important thing for choosing C#.

The environment for your software is most important for choosing C#. If you work in an environment with Windows clients, Windows servers, Active Directory, IIS and maybe SQL Server then C# is the far best language with the .NET Framework.

If you work in a Unix environment with e.g. web services, Java would be my choice. And if you work with embedded systems or have to integrate with hardware devices C++ would be a good choice.

Pro C#:

- garbage collection
- array bounds checking
- huge .NET-Framework library
- types have a defined size (e.g. a long is 64Bit)
- strings are encoded in UTF/16
- autoboxing – every type can be treated as if it inherits from object
- supports constructor-chaining (one constructor can call another constructor from the same class)
- when a virtual method is called in a constructor, the method in the most derived class is used
- static constructors (run before the first instance of the class is created)
- exceptions have access to a stack trace
- advanced runtime type information and reflection

- supports variadic functions nicely
- built-in support for threads
- no need for header files and #includes
- no fall-through on switch-statements
- arithmetic operations can be checked for overflow if required
- objects must have a definite value before being used
- attributes can be attached to classes and retrieved at runtime
- no forward declarations required, classes can be arranged at will
- access to class members / functions is done only by the dot (no more -> or ::)
- conditional functions (e.g. for debugging)
- structs and classes are actually different (structs are value types, have no default constructor in general cannot be derived from)
- supports properties
- readonly members are const, but can be changed in the constructor

- finally block for exceptions
- arrays are objects
- support for anonymous functions
- supports the base keyword for calling the overridden base class

Pro C++

- better performance
- portability
- multiple inheritance
- deterministic destruction (allows RAII)
- any type can be thrown as exception (only classes derived from System.Exception in C#)
- ability to enforce const-correctness
- implicit interfaces on generics (in C#, generics must be constrained with an interface)
- offers pointers (C# only offers pointers in unsafe mode)
- support for macros
- support for global variables, functions, constants

- allows default arguments on function parameters
- STL supports bitfields

Where C# is just different from C++

- value types and reference types exist (struct is value-type, class is reference-type)
- value types live on the stack, reference types on the heap
- references can point to null (must not be valid)
- code is packaged in assemblies in C#
- no automatic conversion from int to bool in C#
- main-function is called Main in C#
- no semicolon after a class declaration in C#
- everything derives from object or can be treated as if

CHAPTER 4

HOW TO INSTALL AND RUN VISUAL STUDIO COMMUNITY

To install the Visual Studio Community 2013, you need to use the following procedure to complete the installation using Windows 8 for the installation, but it holds true for the operating systems mentioned in the prerequisites.

Step 1

Step 2

Click on the Download button and an installer file will start downloading to your system. e following URL [Visual Studio Community 2013] and you will be shown the following screen.

Step 3

After the file is completely downloaded on your
system, click on the file and run the setup. An
important point to note here is Visual Studio
demands a minimum of 9 GB space to be available
somewhere in all your partitions. Please ensure this
requirement to continue with the installation.

Check the "I agree" checkbox and you'll be shown the
Next button on the bottom-right of the wizard. Click
it to proceed.

Step 4

Choose from the following options to install the specific or complete features. It is a best practice to install all the features, still you can choose depending on your requirements and click Install.

Step 5

The installation process takes some time to download the useful resources and other files from the internet to complete the installation depending upon the speed of your internet connection. During my installation, it took just 1 hour to complete the installation.

Step 6

After the setup is finished installing Visual Studio Community 2013 on your machine, it shows the following window. Click on "Launch" to launch Visual Studio.

Step 7

The Welcome screen prompts you to sign in with your Microsoft Account for the first time.

Step 8

Click on "Sign in" and you'll be prompted to enter your login credentials.

Step 9

Log in with your Microsoft credentials and click Sign in. You'll be prompted to create a Visual Studio Online account. You can either choose to create one or skip it by clicking the "Not now, maybe later".

Step 10

Afterwards, you'll be prompted to choose your environment settings. If you're a C# programmer, choose Visual C# as your Development settings. You can also choose your color theme from one of threeoptions.

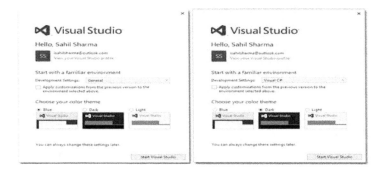

Step 11

When you're done with your development settings, click Start Visual Studio and voila, you are ready to play with the fully functional Visual Studio Community 2013 for free.

CHAPTER 5

BASICS OF C# LANGUAGE

VARIABLE

A variable is an entity whose value can keep changing. For example, the age of a student, the address of a faculty member and the salary of an employee are all examples of variables.

In C# a variable is a location in the computer's memory that is identified by a unique name and is used to store a value. The name of the variable is used to access and read the value stored in it. Various types of data such as a character, an integer or a string can be stored in variables. Based on the type of data that needs to be stored in a variable, variables can be assigned various data types.

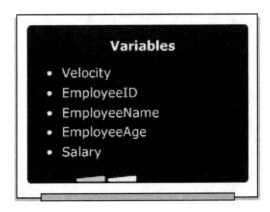

In C#, memory is allocated to a variable at the time of its creation. When you are referring to a variable, you are actually referring to the value stored in that variable.

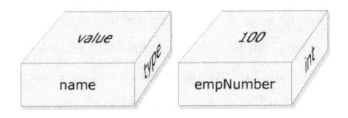

Syntax

The following syntax is used to declare variables in C#:

<Data type> <variable Name>;

Where:

Datatype: Is a valid data type in C#.

VariableName: Is a valid variable name.

The following syntax is used to initialize variables in C#:

<VariableName> = <value>;

=: Is the assignment operator used to assign values.

Value: Is the data that is stored in the variable.

Snippet and Example

The following snippet declares two variables, namely empNumber and empName.

int empNumber;

String empName;

The preceding lines declare an integer variable, empName, and a string variable, empName.

Memory is allocated to hold data in each variable.

Values can be assigned to variables using the assignment operator (=) as shown below.

empNumber=100;

empName="David Blake";

You can also assign a value to a variable upon creation, as shown below.

Int empNumber=100;

Variable Naming Rules

A variable needs to be declared before it can be referenced. You need to follow certain rules when declaring a variable:

A variable name can begin with an upper case or a lower case letter. The name can contain letters, digits and the underscore character (_).

The first character of the variable name must be a letter and not a digit. The underscore is also a legal first character, but it is not recommended at the beginning of a name.

C# is a case-sensitive language; hence the variable names "count" and "Count" refer to two separate variables.

C# keywords cannot be used as variable names. If you still need to use a C# keyword then prefix it with the '@' symbol.

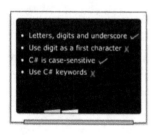

Variable Name	Valid/Invalid
Employee	Valid
student	Valid
_Name	Valid
Emp._Name	Valid
@goto	Valid
static	Invalid as it is a keyword
4myclass	Invalid as a variable cannot start with a digit
Student&Faculty	Invalid as a variable cannot have the special character &

Declaration

In C#, you can declare multiple variables at the same time in the same way you declare a single variable. After declaring variables, you need to assign values to them. Assigning a value to a variable is called initialization. You can assign a value to a variable while declaring it or at a later time. The following code snippet demonstrates how to declare and initialize variables in C#.

```
The following code snippet demonstrates how to declare and
initialize variables in C#.

bool boolTest = true;
short byteTest = 19;
int intTest;
string stringTest = "David";
float floatTest;
intTest =140000;
floatTest = 14.5f;
Console.WriteLine("boolTest = {0}", boolTest);
Console.WriteLine("byteTest = " + byteTest);
Console.WriteLine("intTest = " + intTest);
Console.WriteLine("stringTest = " + stringTest);
Console.WriteLine("floatTest = " + floatTest);

In the above code snippet, variables of type bool, byte, int,
string and float are declared. Values are assigned to each of
these variables and are displayed using the WriteLine()
method of the Console class.
```
Snippet

Constant and its Declaration.

A constant value cannot be changed at compile time and runtime.

Need For Constant

Consider code that calculates the area of a circle. To calculate the area of the circle, the value of PI, ARC, and RADIUS must be provided in the formula. The value of PI is a constant value. This value will remain unchanged irrespective of the value of the radius provided.

Similarly, constants in C# are fixed values assigned to identifiers that are not modified throughout the execution of the code. They are defined when you want to preserve values to reuse them later or to prevent any modification to the values.

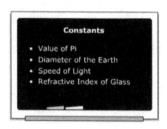

In C#, you can declare constants for all data types. You need to initialize a constant at the time of its declaration. Constants are declared for value types rather than for reference types. To declare an identifier as a constant, the const keyword is used in the identifier declaration. The compiler can identify

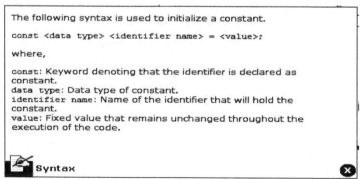

The following syntax is used to initialize a constant.

```
const <data type> <identifier name> = <value>;
```

where,

const: Keyword denoting that the identifier is declared as constant.
data type: Data type of constant.
identifier name: Name of the identifier that will hold the constant.
value: Fixed value that remains unchanged throughout the execution of the code.

Syntax

constants at the time of compilation because of the const keyword.

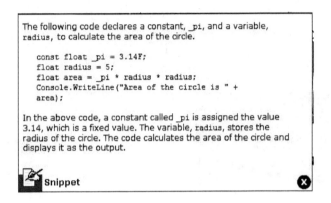

The following code declares a constant, _pi, and a variable, radius, to calculate the area of the circle.

```
const float _pi = 3.14F;
float radius = 5;
float area = _pi * radius * radius;
Console.WriteLine("Area of the circle is " +
area);
```

In the above code, a constant called _pi is assigned the value 3.14, which is a fixed value. The variable, radius, stores the radius of the circle. The code calculates the area of the circle and displays it as the output.

Snippet

Data Types

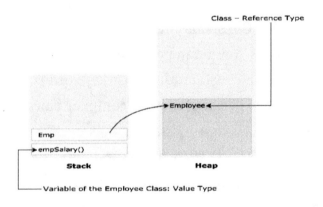

Class – Reference Type

Employee

Emp

empSalary()

Stack   Heap

Variable of the Employee Class: Value Type

You can store various types of values, such as numbers, characters or strings in different variables. But the compiler must know what kind of data a specific variable is expected to store. To identify the type of data that can be stored in a variable, C# provides many data types. When a variable is declared, a data type is assigned to the variable. This allows the variable to store values of the assigned data type. In the C# programming language, data types are divided into two categories. These are:

1. Value Types

Variables of value types store actual values. These values are stored in a stack. The values can be either of a built-in data type or a user-defined data type. Most of the built-in data types are value types. The value type built-in data types are int, float, double, char and bool. Stack storage results in faster memory allocation to variables of value types.

Data Type	Size	Range
byte	Unsigned 8-bit integer	0 to 255
short	Signed 16-bit integer	−32,768 to 32,767
int	Signed 32-bit integer	−2,147,483,648 to 2,147,483,647
long	Signed 64-bit integer	−9,223,372,036,854,775,808 to 9,223,372,036,854,775,807
float	32-bit floating point with 7 digits precision	±1.5e−45 to ±3.4e38
double	64-bit floating point with 15-16 digits precision	±5.0e−324 to ±1.7e308
decimal	128-bit floating point with 28-29 digits precision	±1.0 × 10e−28 to ±7.9 × 10e28
char	Unicode 16-bit character	U+0000 to U+ffff
bool	Stores either true or false	true or false

2. Reference Types

Variables of reference type store the memory address of other variables in a heap. These values can either belong to a built-in data type that is a reference type. Most of the user-defined data types such as class are reference types.

Classification

Reference data types store the memory reference of other variables. These other variables hold the actual values. Reference types can be classified as:

- Object
- String
- Class
- Delegate
- Interface
- Array

Object

Object is a built-in reference data type. It is a base class for all predefined and user-defined data types. A class is a logical structure that represents a real world entity. This means that the predefined and user-defined data types are created based on the Object class.

String

String is a built-in reference type. A String type signifies Unicode character string values. Once strings are created, they cannot be modified.

Class

A class is a user-defined structure that contains variables and methods. For example, the Employee class can be a user-defined structure that can contain variables such as empSalary, empName, and CalculateSalary (), that return the net salary of an employee.

Delegate

A delegate is a user-defined reference type that stores the reference of one or more methods.

Interface

An interface is a type of user-defined class for multiple inheritances.

Array

An array is a user-defined data structure that contains values of the same data type, such as marks as marks of students.

Using Literals

A literal is a static value assigned to variables and constants. You can define literals for any data type of C #. Numeric literals might be suffixed with a letter to indicate the data type of the literal. This letter can be either in upper or lower case. For example, in the following declaration, string bookName = "Csharp", Csharp is a literal assigned to the variable bookName of type string.

In C#, there are six types of literals. These are:

- Boolean Literal
- Integer Literal
- Real Literal
- Character Literal
- String Literal
- Null Literal

1. Boolean Literal

Boolean literals two values, true or false. For example: bool val=true; Where, true: Is a Boolean assigned to the variable val.

2. Integer Literal

An integer literal can be assigned to an int, unit, long or ulong data types. A suffix for integer literals includes U, L, UL, or LU. U denotes unit or ulong, L denotes long. UL and LU denote ulong. For Example: long val = 53L; Where, 53L: Is an integer literal assigned to the variable val.

3. Real Literal

A real literal is assigned to float, double (default), and decimal data types.This is indicated by the suffix letter appearing after the assigned value. A real literal can be suffixed by F, D, or M. F denotes float, D denotes double and M denotes decimal. For example: float val = 1.66F; Where, 1.66F: Is a real literal assigned to the variable val.

4. Character Literal

A character literal is assigned to a char data type. A character literal is always enclosed in single quotes. For example: Char val = 'A'; Where, A: Is a character literal assigned to the variable val.

5. String Literal

There are two types of string literals in C#, regular and verbatim. A regular string literal is a standard string. A verbatim string literal is similar to a regular string literal but is prefixed by the @ character. A string literal is always enclosed in double quotes. For example: String mailDomain = "@gmail.com"; Where, @gmail.com: Is a verbatim string literal.

6. Null Literal

The null literal has only one value, null. For example: String email = null; Where, null: Specifies that email does not refer to any objects (reference)

Keywords

Keywords are reversed words and are separately compiled by the compiler. They convey a predefined meaning to the compiler and hence cannot be created or modified. For example, int is a keyword that specifies that the variable is of data type integer. You cannot use keywords as variable names, method names or class names unless you prefix the keywords with the "@" character. The graphic lists the keywords used in C#:

abstract	bool	break	byte	case	catch
char	class	const	continue	default	double
enum	else	false	finally	float	for
foreach	goto	if	int	interface	long
namespace	new	public	private	protected	return
sbyte	short	static	string	struct	switch
throw	true	try	ushort	void	while

Escape Sequence

An escape sequence character is a special character that is prefixed by a backslash (\). Escape sequence characters are used to implement special non-printing character such as a new line, a single space or a backspace. This non-printing character is used while displaying formatted output to the user to maximize readability. The backslash character tells the compiler that the following character denotes a non-printing character. For example, \n is used to insert a new line similar to the Enter key of the keyboard. There are multiple escape sequence characters in C# that are used for various kinds of formatting. The table shown below displays the escape sequence characters and their corresponding non-printing characters in C#.

Escape Sequence Characters	Non-Printing Characters
\'	Single quote, needed for character literals.
\"	Double quote, needed for string literals.
\\	Backslash, needed for string literals.
\0	Unicode character 0.
\a	Alert.
\b	Backspace.
\f	Form feed.
\n	New line.
\r	Carriage return.
\t	Horizontal tab.
\v	Vertical tab.
\xhh	Matches an ASCII character using hexadecimal representation (exactly two digits). For example, \x61 represents the character 'a'.
\uhhhh	Matches a Unicode character using hexadecimal representation (exactly four digits). For example, the character \u0020 represents a space.

Console Operation

Console operations are tasks performed on the command line interface using executable commands. The console operations are used in software applications because these operations are easily controlled by the operating system. This is because console operations are dependent on the input and output devices of the computer system.

A console application is one that performs operations at the command prompt. All console applications consist of three streams, that are a series of bytes. These streams are attached to the input and output devices of the computer system and they handle the input and output operations. The three streams are:

1. Standard Output method

The standard out stream displays the output on the monitor.

In C#, all console operations are handled by the console class of the system namespace. A namespace is a collection of classes having similar functionalities.

To write data on the console, you need the standard output stream. This stream is provided by the output methods of console class. There are two output methods that write to the standard stream. They are:

Console.Write (): Writes any type of data.

Console.WriteLine (): Writes any type of data this data ends with a new line character in the standard output stream. This means any data after this line will appear on the new line.

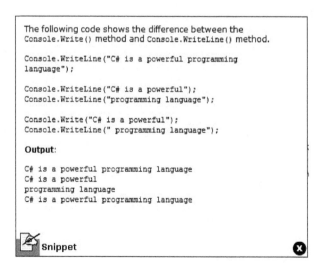

The following code shows the difference between the `Console.Write()` method and `Console.WriteLine()` method.

```
Console.WriteLine("C# is a powerful programming
language");

Console.WriteLine("C# is a powerful");
Console.WriteLine("programming language");

Console.Write("C# is a powerful");
Console.WriteLine(" programming language");
```

Output:

```
C# is a powerful programming language
C# is a powerful
programming language
C# is a powerful programming language
```

Snippet

2. Standard input method

The standard in stream takes the input and passes it to the console application for processing.

In C#, to read data, you need the standard input stream. This stream is provided by the input methods of the console class. These are two input methods that enable the software to take in the input from the standard input stream. These methods are:

Console.Read (): Reads a single character.

Console.ReadLine (): Read a line of strings.

DEMO For ReadMethod

```
namespace ReadMethod

  class Program

    static void Main(string[] args)

      string Name;

      Console.Write("Enter your Name:-");

      Name = Console.ReadLine();
```

```
Console.WriteLine("Your    Name    is:-"    +
Name);

Console.WriteLine("Yoyr    Name    is:-   {0}",
Name);

Console.ReadLine();
```

3. Standard err method

The standard err stream display messages on the monitor.

4. Placeholders

The WriteLine ( ) and Write ( ) methods accept a list of parameters to format text before displaying the output. The first parameter is a string containing markers in braces to indicate the potion where the values of the variables will be substituted. Each marker indicates a zero-based index based on the number of variables in the list. For example, to indicate the first parameter position, you write {0}, second you write {1} and so on. The numbers in the curly brackets are called placeholders.

DEMO For Placeholder

```
namespace Placeholder
  class Program
    static void Main(string[] args)
      int Result, Number;
      Number = 5;
      Result = 100 * Number;
      Console.WriteLine("The result is " + Result +
" when 100 is multiply by" + Number);
      Console.Write("The result is " + Result);
      Console.WriteLine(" when 100 is multiply by "
+ Number);
      Console.WriteLine("The result is {0} when
100 is multiply by {1}", Result, Number);
      Console.ReadLine();
```

5. Convert Methods

The ReadLine () method can be used to accept integer values from the user. The data is accepted as a string and then converted into the int data type. C# provides a convert class base data type.

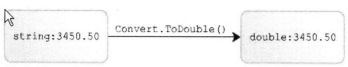

DEMO For ConvertMethod

```
namespace ConvrtMethod
  class Program
    static void Main(string[] args)
          string Name;
      int Age;
      double Salary;
      Console.Write("Enter Your Name:-");
      Name = Console.ReadLine()
      Console.Write("Enter your Age:-");
      Age = Convert.ToInt32(Console.ReadLine());
      Console.Write("Enter your Salary:-");
      Salary                                    =
Convert.ToDouble(Console.ReadLine());
      Console.WriteLine("\nName is :-" + Name);
      Console.WriteLine("Age is :-" + Age);
      Console.WriteLine("Salary is :-" + Salary);
      Console.ReadLine();
```

Programming Constructs or Control-Flow Statement

Welcome to the module C# Programming Constructs. Construct help in building the flow of a program. They are used for performing specific actions depending on whether certain is satisfied repeatedly or can transfer the control to another block.

In this module, you will learn about:

Selection or conditional Statements

Loop Statements

Jump Statements in C#

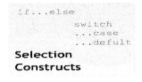

Selection Constructs

Loop Constructs

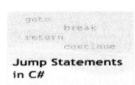

Jump Statements in C#

Selection or Conditional Statements

A selection construct is a programming construct supported by C# that controls the flow of a program. It executes a specific block of statements based on a Boolean condition, that is an expression returning true or false. The selection constructs are referred to as decision-making constructs. Therefore, selection constructs allow you to take logical decisions about executing different blocks of a program to achieve the required logical output. C# supports the following decision-making constructs:

If construct

If..else construct

If..else if construct

Nested if construct

Switch.. case construc

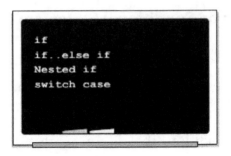

```
if
if..else if
Nested if
switch case
```

1. If construct or statements

The if statement allows you to execute a block of statements after evaluating the specified logical condition. The if statement starts with the if keyword and is followed by the condition. If the condition evaluates to true then the block of statements following the if statement is executed. If the condition evaluates to false then the block of statements following the if statements is ignored and the statement after the block is executed.

If a statement is followed by only one statement then it is not required to include the statement in curly braces.

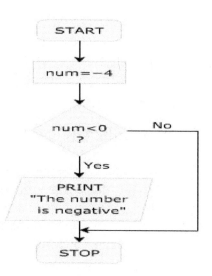

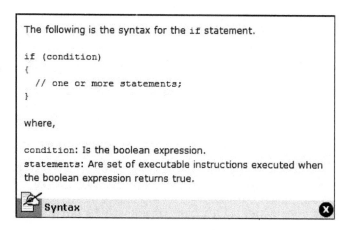

The following is the syntax for the if statement.

```
if (condition)
{
    // one or more statements;
}
```

where,

condition: Is the boolean expression.
statements: Are set of executable instructions executed when the boolean expression returns true.

Syntax

Demo Program

namespace IF_Ststement

  class Program

    static void Main(string[] args)

```
int No1, No2;
Console.WriteLine("Enter Value one:-");
No1 = Convert.ToInt32(Console.ReadLine());
Console.WriteLine("Enter Value second:-");
No2 = Convert.ToInt32(Console.ReadLine());
if (No1 > No2)
    Console.WriteLine("First Value is Big");
        if (No1 < No2)
    Console.WriteLine("Second Value is Big");
Console.ReadLine();
```

2. IF..Else Construct or Statements

The if statements executes a block of statements only if the specified condition is true. However, in some situations, it is required to define an action for a false condition. This is done using the if..else construct.

The if..else construct starts with the if block followed by an else block. The else block starts with the else keyword followed by a block of statements. If the condition specified in the if statement evaluates to false then the statements in the else block are executed.

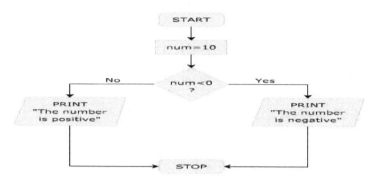

The following is the syntax for the if..else statement.

```
if (condition)
{
    // one or more statements;
}
else (condition)
{
    // one or more statements;
}
```

Syntax ✖

Demo Program

```
namespace IF._._.Else_Statements
  class Program
    static void Main(string[] args)
      int No;
      Console.WriteLine("Enter Any Number:-");
      No = Convert.ToInt32(Console.ReadLine());
      if (No > 0)
        Console.WriteLine("Number is Positive");
```

else

```
Console.WriteLine("Number is Negative");
Console.ReadLine();
```

3. If..Else If Construct or Statements

The if..else if construct allows you to check multiple conditions and it executes a different block of code for each condition. This construct is also referred to as if..else if ladder. The construct starts with the if block followed by one or more else if blocks followed by an optional else block. The conditions specified in the if..else if construct are evaluated sequentially. The execution starts from the if statement. If a condition evaluates to false then the condition specified in the following else if statement is evaluated

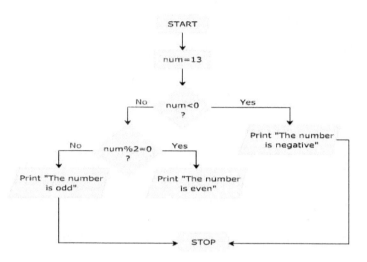

The following is the syntax for the if..else if construct.

```
if (condition)
{
   // one or more statements;
}
else if (condition)
{
   // one or more statements;
}
else
{
   // one or more statements;
}
```

Syntax

Demo Program

```
namespace IF._._ElseIF_Statement
    class Program
        static void Main(string[] args)
            int Num;
            Console.WriteLine("Enter Any Number:-");
            Num = Convert.ToInt32(Console.ReadLine());
            if (Num < 0)
                Console.WriteLine("The      Number      is
Negative");
                else if (Num % 2 == 0)
                Console.WriteLine("The Number is odd");
            else
                Console.WriteLine("The   Number   is
even");
            Console.ReadLine();
```

4. Nested If Construct or Statements

The nested if construct consists of multiple if statements. The nested if construct starts with the if statement, that is called the outer if statements, and contains multiple if statements, that are called inner if statements.

In the nested if construct, the outer if condition controls the execution of the inner if statements. The compiler executes the inner if statements only if the condition in the outer if statements is true. In addition, each inner if statement is executed only if the condition in its previous inner if statement is true.

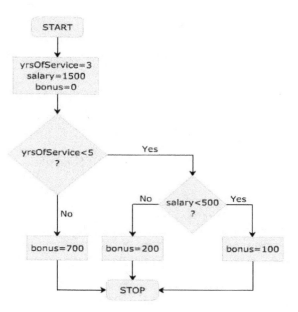

```
The following is the syntax for the nested if construct.

if (condition)
{
        // one or more statements;
        if (condition)
        {
                // one or more statements;
                if (condition)
                {
                        // one or more statements;
                }
        }
}
```

Syntax

Demo Program

namespace Nested_IF_Statement

  class Program

    static void Main(string[] args)

      int Salary, Service;

      Console.Write("Enter Yrs Of Service:-");

      Service   =
Convert.ToInt32(Console.ReadLine());

      Console.Write("Enter Salary:-");

      Salary   =
Convert.ToInt32(Console.ReadLine());

      if (Service < 5)

```
        if (Salary < 500)
    Console.WriteLine("Provided     Bonus:->
100");
        else
    Console.WriteLine("Provided     Bonus:->
200");
        else
        Console.WriteLine("Provided
Bonus:-> 700");
```

5. Switch .. Case Construct or Statements

A program is difficult to comprehend when there are too many if statements representing multiple selection constructs. To avoid using multiple if statements, in certain cases the switch .. case statement can be used as an alternative.

The switch .. case statement is used when a variable needs to be compared against different values.

Switch: The switch keyword is followed by an integer expression enclosed in parentheses. The expression must be of type int, char, byte, or short. The switch statement executes the case corresponding to the expression.

Case: The case keyword is followed by a unique integer constant and a colon. Thus, the case statement cannot contain a variable. The lock following a specific case value match. each case block must end with the break keyword that passes the control out of the switch construct.

Break: The break statement is optional and is used inside the switch .. case statement to terminate the execution of the statement sequence. The control is transferred to the statement after the end of switch. If there is no break then execution flows sequentially into the next case statement. Sometimes, multiple cases can be present without break statements between them.

Default: if no case value matches the switch expression value then the program control is transferred to the default block. This is the equivalent of the "else" of the if..else if construct.

```
switch(expression)
{
case value1:
    //statement sequence
    break;
case value2:
    //statement sequence
    break;
........
........
case valueN:
    //statement sequence
    break;
default:
    //default statement sequence
}
```

Demo Program

namespace Switch_Case

  class Program

    static void Main(string[] args)

      int Day;

      Console.WriteLine("Enter Your Choice:-");

      Day = Convert.ToInt32(Console.ReadLine());

      switch (Day)

        case 1:

          Console.WriteLine("Sunday");

          break;

```csharp
        case 2:
            Console.WriteLine("Monday");
            break;
        case 3:
            Console.WriteLine("Tuesday");
            break;
        case 4:
            Console.WriteLine("Wednesday");
            break;
        case 5:
            Console.WriteLine("Thursday");
            break;
        case 6:
            Console.WriteLine("Friday");
            break;
        case 7:
            Console.WriteLine("Saturday");
            break;
        default:
            Console.WriteLine("Enter    a    Number
between 1 to 7");
            break;
        Console.ReadLine();
```

Loop Construct and Statements

Loops allow you to execute a single statements or a block of statements repeatedly. The most common uses of loops include displaying a series of numbers and tacking repetitive input. In software programming, a loop construct contains a condition that helps the compiler identify the number of times a specific block will be executed. If the condition is not specified then the loop continues infinitely and is called an infinite loop. The loop constructs are also referred to as iteration statements.

C# supports four types of loop constructs. These are:

- The while loop
- The do..while loop
- The for loop
- The foreach loop

1. The "While" Loop

The while loop is used to execute a block of code repetitively as long as the condition of the loop remains true. The while loop consists of the while statement, that begins with the while keyword followed by a Boolean condition. If the condition evaluates to true then the block of statements after the while statement is executed.

After each iteration, the control is transferred back to the while statement and the condition is checked again for another round of execution. When the condition is evaluated to false, the block of statements following the while statement is ignored and the statement appearing after the block is executed by the compiler.

The condition for the while loop is always checked before executing the loop. Therefore, the while loop is also referred to as the pre-test loop.

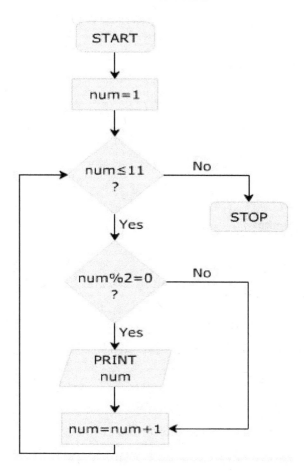

```
The following is the syntax of the while loop.

while (condition)
{
  // one or more statements;
}

where,

condition: Specifies the boolean expression.
```

Syntax ⊗

Demo Program

namespace While_Loop

  class Program

    static void Main(string[] args)

      int num = 1;

      //Console.Write("Enter Number:-");

      //num   =

Convert.ToInt32(Console.ReadLine());

      while (num <= 11)

        if ((num % 2) == 0)

                Console.WriteLine(+num);

      num = num + 1;

      Console.ReadLine();

2. The "Do-While" Loop

The do-while loop is similar to the while loop; however, it is always executed at least once without the condition being checked. The loop starts with the do keyword and is followed by a block of executable statements. The while statement along with the condition appears at the end of this block.

The statements in the do-while loop are executed as long as the specified condition remains true. When the condition evaluates to false, the block of statements after the do keyword are ignored and the immediate statement after the while statement is executed.

The statements defined in the do-while loop are executed for the first time and then the specified condition is checked. Therefore, the do-while loop is referred to as the post-test loop.

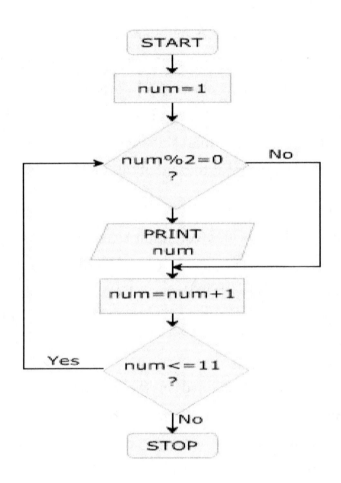

The following is the syntax of the do-while loop.

```
do
{
 // one or more statements;
} while (condition);
```

Syntax ✖

Demo Program

```
namespace DO_While_Loop
  class Program
    static void Main(string[] args)
      int num;
      Console.Write("Enter Number:-");
      num = Convert.ToInt32(Console.ReadLine());
      do
        if ((num % 2) == 0)
          Console.WriteLine(+num);
        num = num + 1;
      while (num <= 11);
      Console.ReadLine();
```

3. The "for" Loop

The for statement is similar to the while statement in its function. The statements within the body of the loop are executed as long as the condition is true. Here too, the condition is checked before the statements are executed

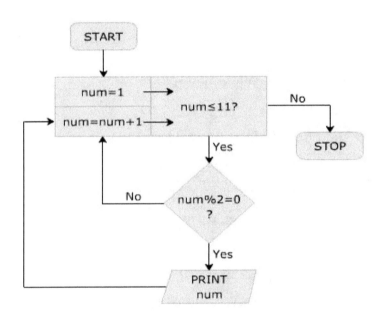

The following is the syntax of the for loop.

```
for (initialisation; condition; increment/decrement)
{
  // one or more statements;
}
```

where,

initialisation: Initializes the variable(s) that will be used in the condition.
condition: Comprises the condition that is tested before the statements in the loop are executed.
increment/decrement: Comprises the statement that changes the value of the variable(s) to ensure that the condition specified in the condition section is reached. Typically, increment and decrement operators like ++, -- and shortcut operators like += or -= are used in this section. Note that there is no semicolon at the end of the increment/decrement expressions.

Syntax   ✖

Demo Program

```
namespace For_Loop

  class Program

    static void Main(string[] args)

        int num, i;

      Console.Write("Enter Number:-");

      num = Convert.ToInt32(Console.ReadLine());

      for (i = num; i <= 11; i++)

        if ((i % 2) == 0)

        Console.WriteLine(+i);

      Console.ReadLine();
```

4. Nested "for" Loop

The nested for loop consists of multiple for statements. When one for loop is enclosed inside another for loop, the loops are said to be nested. The for loop that encloses the other for loop is referred to as the inner for loop.

The outer for loop determines the number of times the inner for loop will be invoked. For each iteration of the outer for loop, the inner for loop executes all its iterations.

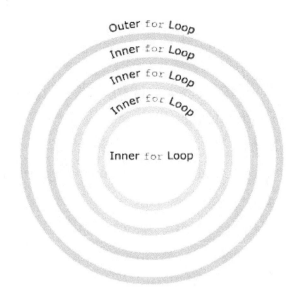

Demo Program

```
namespace Nested_For_Loop
  class Program
    static void Main(string[] args)
      int i, j;
      for (i = 0; i < 5; i++)
        for (j = 0; j < 2; j++)
          Console.WriteLine("Welcome To CCSIT");
      Console.ReadLine();
```

5. The "foreach" Loop

A Foreach loop iterates through the items in the collection

The elements of a collection cannot be modified.

The foreach loop navigates through each value in the specified list and executes the block of statements for each value. The number of values in the list determines how many times the foreach loop will be executed. Each value in the list is referred to as an element. The foreach loop starts with the foreach statements that allows you to specify the identifier that holds a list of values.

While executing the foreach loop, all the elements specified in the for statement become read-only. Therefore, you cannot change the value of any element during the execution of the foreach loop

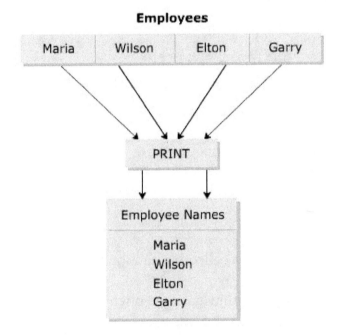

The following is the syntax of the foreach loop.

```
foreach (<datatype> <identifier> in <list>)
{
    // one or more statements;
}
```

where,

datatype:Specifies the data type of the elements in the list.
identifier:Is an appropriate name for the collection of elements.
list:Specifies the name of the list.

Syntax ❌

Demo Program

namespace foreach_Loop

class Program

static void Main(string[] args)

// FOREACH LOOP IS USE FOR STRING

string[] Names = { "joy", "Mariya", "Jeni", "Wilson" };

Console.WriteLine("Employee Name");

foreach (string person in Names)

Console.WriteLine("{0}", person);

```
// FOREACH LOOP IS USE FOR INTEGER

int[] No = { 1, 2, 3, 4 };

Console.WriteLine("\nEmployee Number");

foreach (int Number in No)

    Console.WriteLine("{0}", Number);

Console.ReadLine();
```

Jump Statements

Jump statements are used to transfer control from one point in a program to another. There will be situations where you need to exit out of a loop prematurely and continue with the program. In such cases, jump statements are used. A Jump statement unconditionally transfers control of a program to a different location. The location to which a jump statement transfers control is called the target of the jump statement.

C# supports four types of jump statements. These are:

- Break
- Continue
- Goto
- Return
-

1. Break Statement

The break statement is used in the selection and loop constructs. It is most widely used in the switch .. case construct and in the for and while loops. The break statement is denoted by the break keyword. In the switch .. case construct, it is used to terminate the execution of the construct. In this case, the control passes to the next statement following the loop.

Syntax

```
for (initialisation;condition;increment/decrement)
{
    ...
    if (True Condition)            Quit Loop

            break;
    ...
}
```

Demo Program

namespace Break_Statement

  class Program

    static void Main(string[] args)

      int i;

      double no, sum = 0, avg;

      Console.WriteLine("Enter Number One by One:-");

      Console.WriteLine("Enter Zero to stop Entry");

      for (i = 1; i <= 1000; i++)

        no   = Convert.ToDouble(Console.ReadLine());

        if (no == 0)

          break;

        sum = sum + no;

Console.WriteLine("Sum =>" + sum);

Console.ReadLine();

2. The "continue" Statement

The continue statement is most widely used in loop constructs. This statement is denoted by the continue keyword. The continue statement is used to end the current iteration of the loop and transfer the program control returns back to the beginning of the loop. The statements of the loop following the continue statement are ignored in the current iteration.

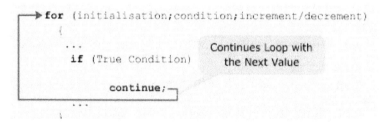

Demo Program

namespace Continue_Statement

  class Program

    static void Main(string[] args)

```
Console.WriteLine("Even numbers in the
range of 1-10");
    for (int i = 1; i <= 10; i++)
        if (i % 2 != 0)
            continue;
        Console.Write(i + "\n");
    Console.ReadLine();
```

3. The "goto" Statement

The goto statement allows you to directly execute a labeled statement or a ladeled block of statements. A labaled is an identifier ending with a colon. A single labeled block can be reffered by more than one goto statements.

The goto statement is denoted by the goto keyword.

You cannot use the goto statement for moving inside a block under the for, while or do-while loops.

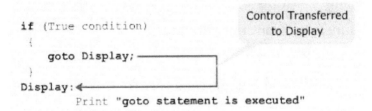

Demo Program

```
namespace Goto_Statement
  class Program
    static void Main(string[] args)
      int i = 0;
    display:
      Console.WriteLine("Hello Word");
      i++;
      if (i < 5)
        goto display;
```

4. The "return" Statement

The return statement returns a value of an expression or transfers control to the method from which the currently executing method was invoked. The return statement is denoted by the return keyword. The return statement must be the last statement in the method block.

```
if (True Condition)
  {
   . . .
      return;
  }
else
  {
   . . .
   . . .
  }
Print "return statement"
```

Program Terminates

Demo Program

namespace Return_Statement

  class Program

    static void Main(string[] args)

      int YrsofService = 5;

      double salary = 1250;

      double bonus = 0;

      if (YrsofService <= 5)

        bonus = 50;

        return;

      else

            bonus = salary * 0.2;

```
        Console.WriteLine("Salary     amount:"    +
salary);
        Console.WriteLine("Bonus     amount:"    +
bonus);
        Console.ReadLine();
```

Statements

Statements are referred to as logical grouping of variables, operators and C# keywords that perform a specific task. For example, the line that initializes a variable by assigning it a value is a statement.

In C#, a statement ends with a semicolon. A program is built with multiple statements and these statements are grouped in blocks. A block is a code consisting of related statements enclosed in curly braces. For example, the set of statements included in the main() method of a C# code is a block.

A method in C# is equivalent to a function in earlier programming languages such as C and C++.

```
class Circle
{
    static void Main(string[] args)
    {
        const float _pi = 3.14F;
        float radius = 5;
        float area = _pi * radius * radius;
        Console.WriteLine("Area of the circle is " + area);
    }
}
```

Block

Statements are used to specify the input, the process and the output takes of a program. Statements can consist of:

- Data types
- Variables
- Operators
- Constants
- Literals
- Keywords
- Escape sequence characters

Statements help you build a logical flow in the program. with the help of statements, you can:

- Initialize variables and objects
- Take the input
- Call a method of a class

- Perform calculations
- Display the output

Example of Statements

```
Example of Statements

int primeNo = 7;
Circle circ = new Circle();
float area = Circ.Area();
int examPercent =
(TotalMarks/600)*100;
Console.WriteLine("Hello");
```

Types of Statements

C# statements are similar to statements in C and C++. C# statements are classified into seven categories depending on the function they perform. These categories are the following.

Selection statements

A selection statement is a decision-making statement that checks whether a specific condition is true or false. The keyword associated with this statement are: if, else, switch and case.

Iteration statements

An iteration statement helps you to repeatedly execute a block of code. The keywords with this statement are: do, for, foreach, and while.

Jump statements

A jump statement helps you transfer the flow from one block to another block in the program. The keywords associated with this statement are: break, continue, default, goto, return.

Exception handling statements

An exception handling statement manages unexpected situations that hinder the normal execution of the program. For example, if the code is dividing a number by zero, the program will not execute properly. To avoid this situation, you can use the following exception handling statements: throw, try-catch, try-finally and try-catch-finally.

Checked and unchecked statements

The checked and unchecked statements manage arithmetic overflows. An arithmetic overflow occurs if the resultant value is greater than the range of the target variable's data type. The checked statement halts the execution of the program whereas the unchecked statement assigns junk data to the target variable. The keywords associated with these statements are: checked and unchecked.

Fixed statement

The fixed statement is required to tell the garbage collector not to move that object during execution. The keywords associated with this statement are: fixed and unsafe.

Lock statement

A lock statement in locking the critical code blocks. This ensures that no locking the critical code. These statements ensure security and only work with reference statements ensure security and only work with reference types. The keyword associated with this statement is: - lock.

Expressions

Expressions are used to manipulation data. Like in mathematics, expressions in programming languages, including C#, are constructed from the operands and operators. An expression statement in C# ends with a semicolon (;).

Expressions are used to:

Produce values.

Produce a result from an evaluation.

From part of anther expression or a statement.

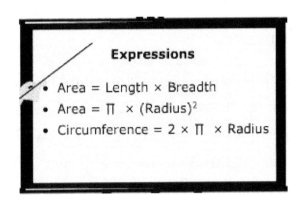

Difference between Statements andExpressions

Statements	Expressions
Do not necessarily return values. For example, consider the following statement: `int oddNum = 5;` The above statement only stores the value 5 in the oddNum variable.	Always return values. For example, consider the following expression: `10000*(75/100)` The above expression returns the value 7500.
Specify the target variable to store the result of computations. For example, consider the following statement: `int evenNum=(10 *100)/5;` The above statement stores the result of the computation in the variable evenNum.	Do not specify the target variable to store the result of computations. For example, consider the following expression: `(8.5+9.4) * (1074.56/6)` The above expression computes a value without storing it in any variable. To store this value, you must assign the expression to a variable. This would require the use of a statement. Expressions, by themselves, do not store values.
Statements are executed by the compiler.	Expressions are part of statements and are evaluated by the compiler.

Introduction to Arrays

An array is a collection of related data with similar data types.

Consider a program that stores the names of 100 students. To store the names, the programmer would create 100 variables of the string type.

Creating and managing these 100 variables is very difficult but the programmer can create an array for storing the 100 names.

An array is a collection of related values placed in a contiguous memory location and these values are referred to using a common array name. This simplifies the maintanance of these values.

Jack	Kate	Francis	Glen	Frank	...

Array of 100 Names

Efficient Memory Utilization

```
//Program to store 100 names of students
string studentOne = "Jack Anderson";
string studentTwo = "Kate Jones";
string studentThree = "Francis Diaz";
string studentFour = "Glen Daniel";
string studentFive = "Frank James";
...
...
... Till 100 variables
```

100 Variables Storing Names

Inefficient Memory Utilization

An array always stores values of a single data type. Each value is referred to as an element. These elements are accessed using subscripts or index numbers that determine the position of the element in the array list.

C# supports zero-based index values in an array. This means that the first array element has index number zero while the last element has index number n-1, where n stands for the total number of elements in the array.

This arrangement of sorting values helps in efficient storage of data, easy sorting of data and easy tracking of the data length.

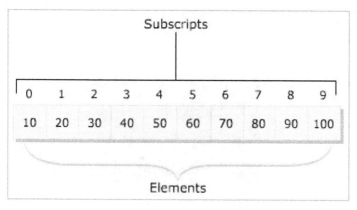

Arrays

Declaration of array

Arrays are reference type variables whose creation involves two steps: declaration and memory allocation.

An array declaration specifies the type of data that it can hold and identifier. This identifier is basically an array name and is used with a subscript to retrieve or set the data value at that location. Declaring an array does not allocate memory to the array.

The following is the syntax for declaring an array.

```
type[] arrayName;
```

where,

type: Specifies the data type of the array elements (for example, int and char).
arrayName: Specifies the name of the array.

Syntax ✕

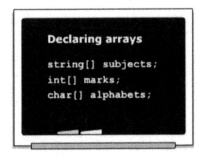

The following is the syntax for declaring an array.

```
type[] arrayName;
```

where,

type: Specifies the data type of the array elements (for example, int and char).
arrayName: Specifies the name of the array.

Syntax ✕

Initializing Arrays

An array can be created using the new keyword and then initialized. Alternatively, an array can be initialized at the time of declaration itself, in which case the new keyword is not used. Creating and initializing an array with the new keyword involves specifying the size of array. The number of elements stored in an array depends upon the specified size. The new keyword allocates memory to the array and values can be assigned to the array.

If the elements are not explicitly assigned then default values are stored in the array. The table shown alongside lists the default values for some of the widely used data types.

Data Types	Default Values
int	0
float	0.0
double	0.0
char	'\0'
string	null

Syntax

Array Syntax

Demo Program

namespace Simple_Array

```
class Program
   static void Main(string[] args)
      int[] count = new int[10];
      int counter = 0, i;
      for (i = 0; i < 10; i++)
         count[i] = counter++;
      Console.WriteLine("The Count value is:-" +
count[i]);
      Console.ReadLine();
```

Types of Arrays

C# .Net mainly has three types of arrays, these are:

Single-Dimension Array.

Multi-Dimension Array.

1. Single-Dimension Array

The elements of a single-dimensional array are stored in a single row in the allocated memory. The declaration and initialization of single-dimensional arrays are the same as the standard declaration and initialization of arrays.

In a single-dimensional array, the elements are indexed from 0 to (n-1), where n is the total number of elements in the array. For example, an array of 5 elements will have the elments indexed from 0 to 4 such that the first element is indexed 0 and the last element is indexed

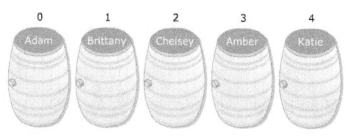

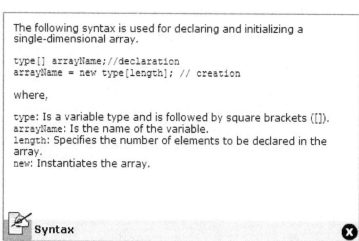

The following syntax is used for declaring and initializing a single-dimensional array.

```
type[] arrayName;//declaration
arrayName = new type[length]; // creation
```

where,

type: Is a variable type and is followed by square brackets ([]).
arrayName: Is the name of the variable.
length: Specifies the number of elements to be declared in the array.
new: Instantiates the array.

Syntax

Demo Program

namespace Simple_Array

  class Program

     static void Main(string[] args)

```
string[] students = new string[3] { "Jems",
"Alex", "Joy" };
    int i;
    for (i = 0; i < students.Length; i++)
       Console.WriteLine(students[i]);
    Console.ReadLine();
```

2. Multi-Dimension Array

Consider a scenario where you need to store the roll number of 50 students and their marks in three exams. Using a single-dimensional array, you require two separate arrays for storing roll numbers and marks respectively. However, using a multi-dimension array, you just need one array to store both, roll numbers as well as marks.

A multi-dimensional array allows you to store combinations of values of a single type in two or more dimensions. The dimensions of the array are represented as rows and columns similar to the rows and columns of a Microsoft Excel sheet.

A multi-dimensional array can have a maximum of eight dimensions.

There are two types of multi-dimensional array, these are:

1.   Rectangular Array.

2.   Jagged Array.

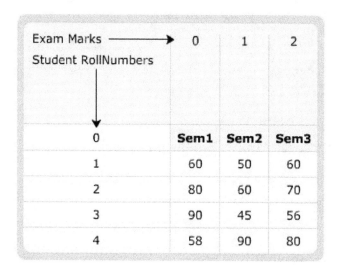

1. Rectangular Array

A rectangular array is a multi-dimensional array where all the specified dimensions have constant values. A rectangular array will always have the same number of columns for each row.

Syntax

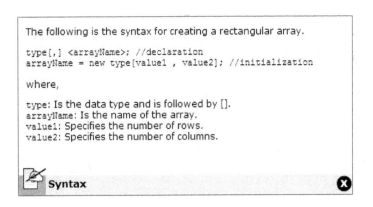

The following is the syntax for creating a rectangular array.

```
type[,] <arrayName>; //declaration
arrayName = new type[value1 , value2]; //initialization
```

where,

```
type: Is the data type and is followed by [].
arrayName: Is the name of the array.
value1: Specifies the number of rows.
value2: Specifies the number of columns.
```

Syntax

Demo Program

```
namespace Multi_Dimensional_array
  class Program
    static void Main(string[] args)
      int[,] dimension = new int[4, 5];
      int numOne = 0;
      for (int i = 0; i < 3; i++)
        for (int j = 0; j < 3; j++)
          dimension[i, j] = numOne;
          numOne++;
      for (int i = 0; i < 3; i++)
```

```
    for (int j = 0; j < 3; j++)
        Console.Write(dimension[i, j] + " ");
    Console.WriteLine();
  Console.ReadLine();
```

2. Jagged Array

A jagged array is a multidimensional array where one of the specified dimensions can have varying sizes. Jagged arrays can have unequal number of columns for each row.

A jagged array is a multi-dimensional array and is referred to as an array of arrays. It consists of multiple arrays where the number of elements within each array can be different. Thus, rows of jagged arrays can have different number of columns.

A jagged array optimizes the memory utilization and performance because navigating and accessing elements in a jagged array is quicker as compared to other multi-dimensional arrays.

For example, consider a class of 500 students where each student has opted for a different number of subjects. Here, you can create a jagged array because the number of subjects for each student varies.

Representation of Jagged Arrays

Demo Program

```
namespace Jagged_Arrays
  class Program
    static void Main(string[] args)
      string[][] companies = new string[3][];
      companies[0] = new string[] { "Intel", "AMD" };

      companies[1]  =  new  string[]  {  "IBM",
"Microsoft", "Sun" };

      companies[2] = new string[] { "HP", "Canon",
"Lexmark", "Epson" };
```

```
    for (int i = 0; i < companies.GetLength(0);
i++)
        Console.Write("List of companies in group"
+ (i + 1) + ":\t");
            for     (int     j     =     0;     j     <
companies[i].GetLength(0); j++)
                Console.Write(companies[i][j]  +
" ");
        Console.WriteLine();
        Console.ReadLine();
```

3. Using the "foreach" Loop for Arrays

The foreach loop in C# is anextension of the for loop. This loop is used to perform specific actions on collections, such as arrays. The loop reads every element in the specified array and allows you to execute a block of code for each element in the array. This is particularly useful for reference types, such as strings.

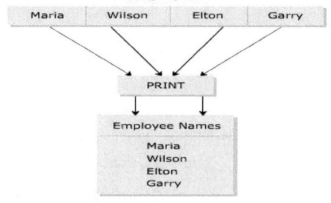

The following is the syntax of the foreach loop.

```
foreach (<datatype> <identifier> in <list>)
{
    // one or more statements;
}
```

where,

datatype:Specifies the data type of the elements in the list.
identifier:Is an appropriate name for the collection of elements.
list:Specifies the name of the list.

Syntax

Demo Program

```
namespace Foreach_Loop_For_Array

class Program

static void Main(string[] args)
```

```
string[] studentNames = new string[3] {
"JAY", "MAHESH", "RAJ" };

foreach (string studName in studentNames)

    Console.WriteLine("Congratulations!!  " +
studName + " You Have Selected for This Job");

    Console.ReadLine();
```

Type Casting

Consider the payroll system of an organization. The gross salary of an employee is calculated and stored in a variable of float type. Currently, the output is shown as float values. The payrll department wants the salary amount as a whole number and thus wants any digits after the decimal point of the calculated salary to be ignored. The programmer is able to do this using the typecasting feature of C#. Typecasting allows you to change the data type of a variable.

C# supports two types of casting, namely implicit and explicit. Type casting is mainly used to:

Convert a data type to another data type belonging to the same or a different hierarchy. For example, the numaric hierarchy includes int, float and double. You can convert the char type into int type to display the ASCII value.

Display the exact numeric output. For example, you can display exact quotionts during mathematical divisions.

Prevent loss of numaric data if the resultant value exceeds the range of its variable's data type.

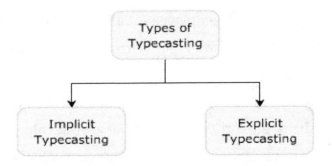

1. Implicit Conversions for C# Data Types

Implicit typecasting refers to an automatic conversion of data types. This is done by the C# compiler. Implicitly typecasting is done only when the destination and source data types belong to the same hierarchy. In addition, the destination data type must hold a larger range of values than the source data type. Implicit conversion prevents the loss of data as the destination data type is always larger than the source data type. For example, if you have a value of int type then you can assign that value to the variable of long type.

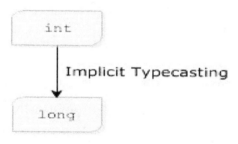

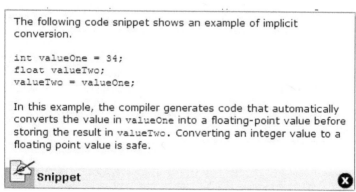

The following code snippet shows an example of implicit conversion.

```
int valueOne = 34;
float valueTwo;
valueTwo = valueOne;
```

In this example, the compiler generates code that automatically converts the value in valueOne into a floating-point value before storing the result in valueTwo. Converting an integer value to a floating point value is safe.

Snippet

Demo Program

namespace Implicit_TypeCasting

  class Program

```
static void Main(string[] args)
int valOne = 20;
int valTwo = 30;
float valThree;
valThree = valOne + valTwo;
Console.WriteLine("Addition of Two
variables:-" + valThree);
Console.ReadLine();
```

Rules

Implicit typecasting is done automatically by the compiler. The C# compiler automatically converts a lower precision data type into a higher precision data when the target variable is of a higher precision than the source variable.

The graphic illustrates the various data types and the data types of higher precision to which they can be converted.

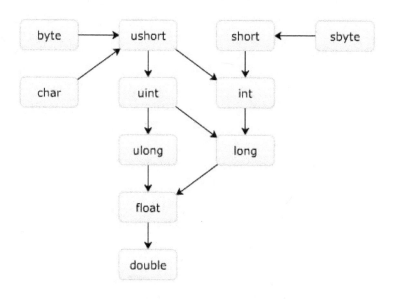

2. Explicit Conversions for C# Data Types

Explicit typecasting refers to changing a data type of higher precision into a data type of lower precision. For example, using explicit type casting, you can manually convert the value of float type into int type. This typecasting might result in loss of data. This is because when you convert the float data type into the int data type, the digits after the decimal point are lost.

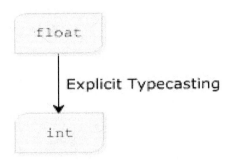

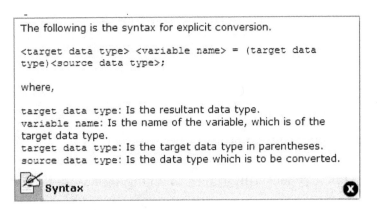

Demo Program

namespace Implicit_Typecasting

  class Program

    static void Main(string[] args)

      float side = 10.5F;

      int area;

      area = (int)(side * side);

Console.WriteLine("Area of the Squre = {0}", area);

Console.ReadLine();

Boxing and Unboxing

Boxing and unboxing are concepts of C# data type system. Using these concepts, a value of any value type can be converted to a reference type and a value of any refeerance type can be converted to a value type.

Boxing

Boxing is a process for converting a value type, like integer, to its reference type, like objects. This convertion is useful to reduce the overhead on the system during execution. This is because all value types are implicitly of object type.

To implement boxing, assign the value type to an object. While boxing, the variabe of the value type variable. This means that the object type has the copy of the value instead of its reference.

Boxing is done implicitly when a value type is provided instead of the expected reference type.

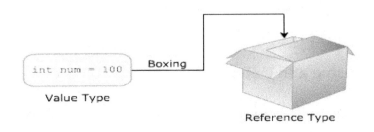

The following is the syntax for boxing.

object <instance of the object class> = <variable of value type>;

where,
object: Is the base class for all value types.
instance of the object class: Is the name referencing the Object class.
variable of value type: Is the identifier whose data type is of value type.

Syntax

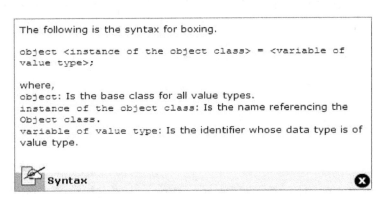

Demo Program

namespace Boxing_Type

   class Program

      static void Main(string[] args)

         // Demo-1

         int radious = 10;

         double area;

```
area = 3.14 * radious * radious;
object boxed = area;
Console.WriteLine("DEMO-1 OUTPUT\n");
Console.WriteLine("Area    of    the    circule=
{0}\n", area);
//Demo-2
double bonus = 0.0;
double salary;
Console.WriteLine("DEMO-2 OUTPUT\n");
Console.WriteLine("Enter Salary:-");
salary                              =
Convert.ToDouble(Console.ReadLine());
bonus = salary * 0.1;
object any = bonus;
Console.WriteLine("Bonus    of    Rs.{0}    is
Rs.{1}", salary, bonus);
Console.ReadLine();
```

Unboxing

Unboxing is a process for converting a reference type, like objects, to its value type, like integer. This conversion is useful to reduce the overhead on the system during execution. This is object type because all are implicitly of value types.

To implement unboxing, assign the reference type to an value type. While unboxing, the reference is of the reference type variable. This means that the value type has the copy of the value instead of its value.

Unboxing is done implicitly when a reference type is provided instead of the expected value type.

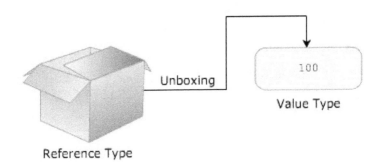

Unboxing

Value Type

Reference Type

The following is the syntax for unboxing.

```
<target value type> <variable name> = (target value
type) <object type>;
```

where,

target value type: Is the resultant data type.
variable name: Is the name of the variable of value type.
target value type: Is the resultant value type in parentheses.
object type: Is the reference name of the Object class.

Syntax

Demo Program

```
namespace UnBoxing_Type
    class Program
        static void Main(string[] args)
            //Demo-1
            int length = 10;
            int breadth = 20;
            int area;
            area = length * breadth;
            object boxed = area;
            int num = (int)boxed;
            Console.WriteLine("DEMO-1 OUTPUT\n");
            Console.WriteLine("Area of the
Rectangle={0}\n", num);
```

```csharp
//Demo-2
double bonus = 0.0;
double salary;
Console.WriteLine("DEMO-2 OUTPUT\n");
Console.WriteLine("Enter Salary:-");
salary =
Convert.ToDouble(Console.ReadLine());
bonus = salary * 0.1;
object any = bonus;
double num2 = (double)bonus;
Console.WriteLine("Bonus of Rs.{0} is
Rs.{1}", salary, bonus);
Console.ReadLine();
```